Constable

Vasile Nicolescu

ABBEY LIBRARY
LONDON

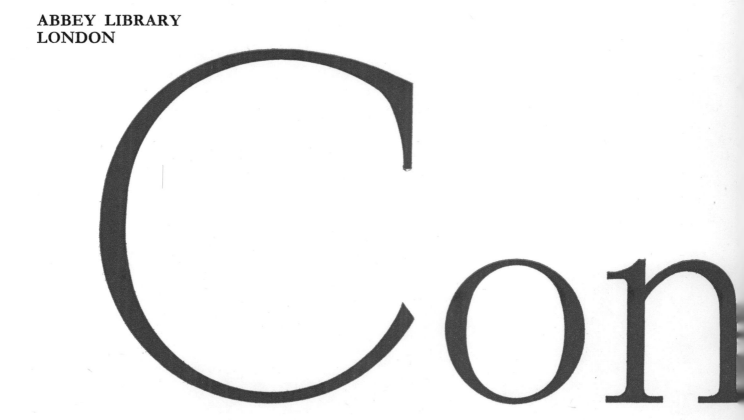

stable

Translated from Romanian as published by
MERIDIANE PUBLISHING HOUSE
Bucharest, 1977
under the original title of
CONSTABLE
by
VASILE NICOLESCU

Translated into English by
ANDREEA GHEORGHIŢOIU

*Painting is with me but another word
for feeling.*

CONSTABLE

The universe of English art, candidly and dramatically unique, has caused many a metaphorical or routine questions to be asked. What archaic residues, what archetypal substrata — Celtic, Anglo-Saxon or Norman — were prevalent in determining and establishing the basic elements of English art? What are the elements that can reveal more strikingly the significant course taken by its artistic sensitiveness?

It was often enough that alongside these questions some people also held — an erroneous, hardly acceptable opinion — that as the English could not fully express themselves in music and through music, they made up for it in the vehement or ethereal chromatics of the landscapes, in the exhuberant solar canvases of the great landscape painters in which colour plays an outstanding role. Starting from this critical impression, one could hold — the fact is not too difficult to demonstrate — that English poetry which so often eulogized music — directly or in a roundabout way — contains in its very fibres (we are referring to Shakespeare, Shelley, Keats or Eliot) even more music, more *sonorous depths*, a more harmonious ineffable character than English painting. Shall we then venture to speak about English music? We do not wish to repeat things already known. Everybody knows there is music indeed in the works of Dunstable Dowland, Byrd, Purcell, Elgar, Vaughan, Williams, who through their vocal or liturgical creations, through sonatas, theatre music, ballets or concertos, contributed masterpieces to the history of the most abstract and serious of arts.

Between the sacred monody or the Gregorian chant and Britten's subtle yet simple constructions one can find the various stages of development of an original and highly important chapter in the history of world music.

The idea of some continental exegetes who consider the English landscape painting (in fact the most enduring and characteristic aspect of Albion's painting) the expression of a compensatory element that the English are strongly aware of deep down in their heart haunted as it is by the furious ocean, by the mysterious mists of the North, by the all-powerful fogs, this idea is more plausible, and in any case deserves more attention in the effort to reveal a prevalent vein of sensitiveness.

Viewed in this light, the English landscape painting appears to the English spirit as a sort of compensation, as its liberating sign. Though a means of poetic expression through colour, the landscape cannot be said to possess one single dimension only. The English landscape, the same as any other, meets first and foremost a profound need for communication, a vital need any human being feels when coming into contact with the elements, with the human element itself. If we grounded it on strictly

5

compensatory explanations, which are sure to be simplifying, how could we appreciate the Dutch landscape paintings, for example Coninxloo's woodlands with their mythological spaciousness, Jacob van Ruisdael's mills with their water-like coloured crystal? How could we appreciate the so-called *Genesis of Vienna*, the frescoes with subjects taken from the Odissey at the Vatican Museum, made about A.D. 560 in Antioch by the miniature painter known as "the illusionist"; or Canaletto's landscapes with the sharp contours of the gondolas cut out with a razor as it were and bathed in an "everlasting" light, Guyp's and Aivazovski's seascapes, the delicate tints of Utamaro's colour prints, the cosmic swirling evanescence in Turner's last paintings or the landscapes belonging to Grigorescu's so-called *white period*, the canvases painted with "honey" by Watteau, the irridiscent and generously imanent golden hues on the large surfaces painted by Claude Lorrain, the light absorbed by the dusky twilight in some of Whistler's canvases? How could we appreciate them when the landscape has always been *a state of mind*, a mood of the human spirit, a parcel of man's moral make-up? In any case a landscape is neither correct static description, nor pure decoration, nor again a diorama or a photograph. The real landscape transcends the facile equilibrium we find in some serially produced paintings with certain elements of nature, hastily called *landscapes*. The allegory of *Good and Bad Government*, a fresco by Ambrogio Lorenzetti, is also a landscape. The same is Beethoven's *Pastoral*, the same are some infernal or heavenly Dantesque hallucinations, the oneiric parts in *Kubla Khan* by Coleridge or *The Ghosts* by the Romanian poet Mihai Eminescu, as also the landscape described by Tudor Arghezi or those, reflexive and bitter, by Henri Michaux:

> *"Calm and desolate landscapes.*
> *Landscapes suggesting the roads of life*
> *rather than the face of the earth,*
> *Landscapes of Time flowing slowly,*
> *almost imperceptibly, so slowly*
> *that it seems to recede.*
> *Landscapes of shreds, of shredded nerves, of "saudade"*
> *Landscapes that heal wounds, steel, brilliance,*
> *evil, time, the noose round people's necks,*
> *and any call to arms.*
> *Landscapes meant to smother cries."*

It is the intuition of Kenneth Clark — a famous English theoretician — that leads us to such an interpretation when he subjects Bruegel's work to a vibrant profound analysis suggesting an integrating vision. Clark holds that Bruegel starts with proverbs and allegories in which the landscape is only a setting or a subsidiary element to go on subsequently to the great landscapes in which the various episodes of man's life are at one with the weather and the seasons. Few works of art can do without a commentary. Like Haendel's oratorio *Messiah* or Bunyan's *Pilgrim's Progress*, Bruegel's landscapes are some of the few masterpieces whose appeal is as universal as it is direct. Further on, Kenneth Clark adds that the confidence with which Bruegel looks back and forth in time, using all the weapons he can lay hands on, is almost Shakespearian and springs from a similar aim: to express a general sympathy for mankind. For despite the fact that all the human beings he paints (whose faces are reduced to simple discs) seem to lose any individual character and become only parts of a universal mechanism, it is their struggle, their sufferings and few physical pleasures that in the end captivate Bruegel.

The landscape is often a transitional space, serving to pass imperceptibly from one stage to another, from one light into another. The landscape marks the entrance into and emergence from the real. Its presence is felt at the beginning and the end of a dream. It is the bridge spanning them. It is the privileged moment of the contemplation of the inner convergence with the light of the real. Marcel Proust had found the magic key to these possible fusions, the sensorial code of some memorable correspondences: "Espousing the form of the hill, associated to the taste of chocolate and to all the texture of my thoughts at the time, the fog, though I never gave it a thought, came to drown all my thoughts at that time, or, unchangeable and massive, it had clung to my impressions of Balbec, or, like the near presence of the exterior staircase of blackish stone, it lent some grey tincture to my impressions of Combray."

Windmill on East Bergholt Heath

Performing many a time a symbolic function, a mirror raised in a dream over the clouds and turned down so as to concentrate all the solar radiations on its surface and reflect the shady folds of the earth, of existence, the English landscape has become a subject of meditation on the inexhaustible beauty of nature and the world.

When trying to solve the mystery of the flourishing of the English landscape painting in the 19th. century, we cannot ignore the contribution of some continental "experiences", without overlooking, however, the artistic sensitiveness we have already mentioned, the refined expression, the trained eye, the progress made by some painting techniques.

The Dutch landscape was one of the English painters' great obsessions. A school and an altar, a field of experience, a secret attraction confessed or not, the Dutch landscape has always fascinated them. "I have seen this morning a moving picture by Ruisdael, it *is haunting me*," Constable was to write towards the end of his life. They were equally fascinated by Claude Lorrain, the French Homer of landscape painting. Turner, for instance, was all his life filled with the ambition of excelling him. It is common knowledge that, before his death, Constable made copies after Claude Lorrain. The Venetian and Italian landscape painting represented by Canaletto, Guardi, Salvator Rosa, Giorgione reveals their *obsession* in this respect. Prompted by it, Turner went to Italy and came back with his prodigious water-colours *Bridge with Tower at Spoleto, Moonlight on the Lagoon, Venice, Sailing Ship* and others, in which he achieved an unusual inner harmony, and trying to advocate, as Marcel Brion believes, "an aesthetics of the static, the unending happy peace Italy offered foreign artists."

All these options, lessons, refusals, clashes and confrontations helped English landscape painting to gain ground. The progress was so great that many were those who, later on, were to acknowledge irrefutably its shaping influence upon the art of the continental landscape, upon the great revolution European art went through in the second half of the 19th century with the emergence of Impressionism.

Between moments of humiliating peace (Versailles 1783) and the victory of Trafalgar, in the moments of panic caused by the victory of the French Revolution and the recognition of the independence of the American colonies as well as the retrocession of some islands to Spain, in the moment of shallow apotheosis when, in 1801, Ireland was united to England to form the United Kingdom of Great Britain and Wellington's success over Napoleon I, England became aware — more than ever before — of her depths, abysses, roots, ambitions, élans, vanities and hopes. The constitutional government under Pitt the Younger — more active and mobile, more realistic than the one headed by his father — the ideas in the new law of economic reform advocated by Burke (the same man who, an extremist and Tory himself was to attack the French Revolution), the democratic ideas of Tom Paine who was able to detect the first effects of a wider democratic movement stimulated by the ever greater proportions assumed by the Industrial Revolution, the violence of the anti-Jacobin Toryisms, the withdrawals of the Whig Party, all these facts and developments were to impress the whole English sensitiveness. England went through the most contradictory hypostases, calmly and enthusiastically, with apathy or fervour, encouraging extravagance or ignoring it, encouraging oratory or sarcastically beheading it, oscillating between extreme lucidity and an unprecedented historical narcissism.

The fierce prosaic character of life, minutely realistic and calculating, combines with the delirious escape from the real. Horace's *otium* alternates with the need for adventure, with the seeking of the unexpected, of the mysterious, with exaltation or dreams. Shelley couches in the cadences of the *Ode to the West Wind* the feeling of the inexorable return of universal spring, the impossibility of reverting to the old order of things; he attacks the programmatic reactionarism of a Castlereagh and expresses his exultant joy in *Prometheus Unbound*, a poem which is much more than a parable of liberty. Byron fights a revolutionary fight on the battlefield at Missolonghi impressing the whole world through the sacrifice of his life. Platonic contemplation holds sway in Keat's golden lines *A thing of Beauty is a joy for ever* (Endymion). Wordsworth preaches, Rousseau-like, the return to nature and cultivates even a mysticism of nature.

Against this background of historic convulsions and romantic outbursts, the aesthetic of the picturesque was gaining ground, facilitating the appearance of the landscape painting of a Gainsborough as well as the development of the genre illustrated by Wilson, Crome, Cozens, Cotman, Blake, Stubs. The impetuous succession of events often calls for the counterpoint of contemplation. People find themselves at a crossroad; on the Continent the author of Faustus feels he must exclaim before the moment: "Oh, don't go, you are so beautiful!" A reflex of the simple and natural inclination of the English heart to reverie, the landscape becomes widely diversified and is patterned on the source of inspiration and on the temperamental make-up of the painters. There is a visionary landscape, openly lyrical, evincing an impetuous imagination, never curbed by the rigours of the genre; and there is also the classical landscape with mythological elements in it. There is the delicate ornamental landscape that expresses the feelings of less selective minds in the arrangement and presentation of images, as there is also the landscape which suggests an atmosphere or a dramatic tension, which eliminates the raw elements of the real and preserves only the essential through a superior recomposition. While in poetry the genius for the language can be expressed in the form of a sonnet and in music in the form of a rondo, the landscape in painting is an eloquent species through which the human genius manifests itself.

However, no matter the medium used (oil, gouache, watercolour or aquatint, achieved in the most unusual techniques) landscape painting when meeting great inspiration and the pure sources of imagination reaches the sublime. As it often happens with great personalities, Constable profited by the technical gains of this art as well as by the favourable moral atmosphere of the genre.

Not so collected perhaps or so silent, so gravely sullen and reserved as he appears to be when we compare him with Turner, his enthusiastic contemporary, Constable, with a less visible and therefore more stubborn tenacity, can gradually find the mystery of colour, its tangible substance. Turner, who wrote poetry too, clothes his heart in a rainbow and dreams of the alchemy of colours, mixes them, tests their effects in diagrams, paints — as it has been said — with coloured vapour, with air even. He wishes to achieve the impossible feat of sticking his retina to the lightning, he lets himself be lashed by sleet and storm with eyes wide open, wishing—superbly romantic—to "steal" the demiurgic secret of the elements. Less spectacular, Constable clothes his spirit in the rough or oily matter of his paints, he is haunted by the germinative fluid of the universe, seeks the live root of colour, calmly hides inside everlasting nature, to be able to last himself. He is the humble apostle of nature, of a reviving nature. Turner is a rebellious Prometheus, a wily impetuous creature in the face of mystery. A pantheist, Constable looks at some mill-race with the startled eye of the man who would look at the Genesis of things. Only a piercing, enthusiastic mind, such as Ruskin's could intuit the personality of the landscape painter when he wrote that "in a landscape Constable feels that the grass is wet, the meadows smooth, the branches shady, in other words almost as much as a fawn or a skylark could feel." Without Cyclopean visions or phantastic haloes, without Turner's cosmic ambit, withdrawn in contemplation, in the boundless sincerity of contemplation, more "Dutch", Constable reaches the sublime of great art. The simple grandeur of his landscapes, his structural harmony, achieved by apparently usual means, make us come into contact with the *Secret*, with the organic beauty of the world. You must only gaze at the "suites" of "clouds" in the Victoria and Albert Museum or at the cloudy efflorescence in other canvases to feel the modulation and sense of his reverie. You have only to gaze at the drowsy and dreamy water in *Water-Meadows near Salisbury*, at the airy density — if we may term it so — of the aquatic element in which the dark green tree-tops along the bank are floating upside down, to realize how true — how perfectly valid for the sensitiveness of the painter — are Gaston Bachelard's remarks concerning the limits of reverie: "He will always go a little beyond the real. Such is the phenomenologic law of poetic reverie. Poetry continues the beauty of the world, 'aesthetizes' the world." Always burning, Constable's devout and sound emotivity recomposes and continues the beauty of the world in the beauty of his palette.

Like most romantics Constable never felt the impulse of great calls, the flight from reality, the fascination of mythology, of unknown climes or seas. Starting from such facts, an oversimplified, naively contrastive view reveals a robust, apparently prosaic nature lacking the idealism of a tortured personality, restless and dramatic.

In the eye of a romantic biographer, Constable led an almost peaceful uneventful life, marked by none of the outward signs of the extraordinary. However, when examining it more closely and unbiasedly we have the revelation of an existential compact life, of a simple life — but all the more fully experienced — a life unfolding itself like a ritual, the life of a man who valued the effort to develop and perfect his talent through hard strenuous work. The son of a miller living in the village of East Bergholt, Suffolk, the painter lived from a child in close communion with a radiant nature which always appealed to his eye, to his sensitivity and aroused his interest. His native Suffolk scenery was to the startled retina of the child, a masterful painting drawn with sweeping gestures in broad strokes by an invisible hand. These natural paintings — profound, restful, replete with some mysterious hope — found a deep echo in his heart as he

The Artist's Children playing the Coach Driver

was to confess later: "I associate my 'careless boyhood' to all that lies on the banks of the Stour . . . They made me a painter . . . that is, I had often thought of pictures of them before I had ever touched a pencil." Possessed as it were by the demon of painting, Constable felt an early need for thorough self-knowledge, for fulfilment. Thanks to his mother's careful endeavours he was presented to Sir George Beaumont, a philanthropist of the time — a man we can meet in the life of other painters as well — who helped him get acquainted with Thomas Girtin's water-colours and with Claude Lorrain's *Expulsion of Hagar*. The emotion he felt when he first encountered Lorrain was tremendous.

While his personality was being shaped, Constable could not, for the moment, avoid the signs of failure and crisis: Smith, a London engraver who gave correspondence lessons, advised him to give up painting. Dwelling on this moment in the painter's life, J. J. Mayoux wrote the following: "Even before this fatal verdict, he *(i.e. Smith)* had shown him how important it was and how difficult to render light in movement or, more exactly, light vibrating on the surface of "picturesque" objects . . . Smith showed him how important the various shades of green were and revealed Gainsborough to him, his fellow countryman who was to be one of his 'interceding saints'".

The discovery of the Dutch painters Ruisdael and Hobbema, as well as of Rubens, greatly fired his imagination. The keen eye of the painter discovered the strict laws governing Hobbema's landscapes more particularly. Following a letter of recommendation by Joseph Farrington (a pupil of Richard Wilson) he attended the Royal Academy School (1799). His first confrontation with the critics' opinions after sending a landscape painting to the summer Salon of the Academy strengthened his determination to define his personality. On the other hand, the gentle, intimate, almost Franciscan naturalism he discovered in Wordsworth's poetry, the strong temptation he felt to turn to the pure sources of nature, the pathos of nature, all this plunged him in deep meditation and determined him to make a decision consonant to his temperament: "I shall return to Bergholt where I shall endeavour to get a pure and unaffected manner of representing the scenes that may employ me... There is room for a natural painter." He also held that truth is the only thing we are left with. An alien to the development of the time, unwilling or perhaps unable to make out their convulsions, an alien to the spasms of his contemporary history, to the grandeur and decline of certain institutions or ideals, rejecting pose and stiffness, showing no interest in mundane affairs, Constable sought refuge in a simple, domestic life, a life of hard work and firm inner discipline. At the age of 33 he proposed to Maria Bricknell and became

Study of Plants   *Sky Study*

engaged to her. They could not get married for a time as for six years running the girl's parents refused to give their consent.

The early years of his married life were the period of a rich undreamt of creative activity for the painter who had harboured such sad illusions in his heart, such melancholy expectations. It was the time of an "uninterrupted" activity, when his artistic creation was the most solar and enthusiastic *(Flatford Mill on the River Stour* was not the only instance). The fame he won after his rather unwilling participation in the great Paris exhibition of 1824 where his *Hay Wain* was on show did not turn his attention away from the necessity he felt permanently to renew his language in order to acquire an absolute freedom in the use of his means of expression. However his wife's illness and death in 1828, a tragical moment in his life, found him completely defenceless. It was only his stubborn determination to keep his balance that helped him avoid a breakdown, perhaps his deep love for his seven children too and the force of his talent, the purifying illusion of creation, the hope which never abandoned him that he would succeed. The examination of his work reveals the mechanisms of sensitivity which the life of the artist — as far as we know it — does not show.

A distinguished self-taught artist, Constable expressed in his work a loftily poetic and humane spiritual experience. When closely examined and interpreted — after the great experiments of a Corot, the pictorial victories of Monet and the various searchings of modern art — Constable's manner of painting appears today infinitely richer in its poetic resources, in its power of concentrating and expressing the essential in nature, in the simple charm which delights the eye. Secretly despising the torpor of those who carry on useless experiments and are fond of abstract hieroglyphs, condensing the language of his art, the Suffolk painter is both a realist and a romantic, an uncommonly complex personality. He perfectly set off any detail, but he was always mindful of truthfulness and rhythm, careful to achieve deep perspective, to render the vividness of the ensemble. On the other hand the structure of his paintings recalls the studied polyphony of the great masters of colour. Jean Pierre Richard's remarks on a Proustian landscape in the novel *A la recherche du temps perdu* seem to disclose some of the mystery of Constable's painting: "A light coloured touch betrays a deep accumulation of energy . . . this is the abundant flow, the inner mobilization of heavy ponderous material elements, which eventually generate the tint." Indeed, the dramatic character of Constable's painting is condensed in the most baffling harmony. It is not enough to paint storms in order to be dramatic. It is not enough to come into clash with your own time, with society, with its inertia and prejudices in order to be dramatic indeed. Constable was able to understand that it is not the subject that proves the excellence of talent in art but the line followed by sentiment, the sense of vision, the means, the ability to organize the masses of colour, the gift of concentrating the effects, of stressing the vigorous tones from within and of imperceptibly bringing out their vivid reliefs or balanced mat quality. By way of illustration let us mention the motif of the storm, which always arrested his attention; besides, some of his exegetes consider *Hadleigh Castle* "his most spontaneous and most naturally tragic painting," likening it to the hallucinating *Cornfield with Crows* by Van Gogh. He could paint with a consummate skill fantastic skies, tenebrous chasms, towers and cliffs portending terror. A contemporary of Coleridge and Blake, of Fuseli's or Palmer's experiments, he could not avoid the climate of his epoch. Yet his work, even when evincing an inclination to the fantastic, reached its full development at the opposite pole, firmly anchored in a fresh and warm spiritual environment in which the sun, the symbol of light is the supreme governing principle of the universe. The painter of joy, joy felt when rendering the bark of a tree (an infinite of luminous reverberations of matter), joy when exalting the transparency of water, joy in the folding clouds moving as it were in a dream, joy in spreading the deep mineral green in *Wivenhoe Park*, Constable, like the romantic poet Thomson, the author of *Summer*, reveals to us nature's secret smile, a sthenic illusion of the final harmony of all things.

Both spontaneous and studied when handling colour, Constable felt drawn to express himself by sincerity and freshness rather than by the illusion of a cold abstract perfection. It is his *pochades*, the studies he made in preparation for the finished works that make a stronger impression on us today. (Needless to say that his 'sketches' were no simple rapid improvisations made on the spot, but succesive reflections of his great reveries, the signs of his dramatic fight with the "demon" of light, with the unseen). That is why we are impressed by the way in which Aurélien Digeon "reads" Constable's temperamental technique when he rightly sees in the painter's work: "On the one hand an impetuous, passionate work which still astonishes the onlooker today (even after Impressionism, even after Van Gogh) by its almost brutal vitality, by the inexhaustible vibration of its colouring and light, on the other hand a more sedate sketch, a muted and 'finished' sketch in every detail. The latter may rouse our admiration even more if one had not seen the first, which the catalogues name 'a last study for the finished composition'. In my opinion one must not hesitate to consider these *studies*, these sketches, the real original compositions, 'my real paintings', while the others are 'replicas to the taste of the public at large'." This seems to be a question of strict craftsmanship but we cannot consider it indifferently. Any critic attempting a conforming analysis of Constable's work will always hold that the best paintings are those *finished* and not vice versa. However, clear-sighted art critics have also maintained that most of

12

Constable's canvases do not evince a complete finish, for the painter reserved for himself the right to reconsider every motif, every pictorial idea over and over again. In fact was there any great master able to put the last finishing touches to his pictures? Heredia's *Les Trophées* or Gautier's *Emaux et Camées* may be finished, rounded off, completed, but we cannot imagine there is any great master to have come to the conclusion that he has definitively completed his work ... Despite its perfection is Michelangelo's *Last Judgement* finished? Are Brancusi's *Maiastras* finished? Any perfection or completion is relative and perhaps this accounts for the hidden charm of some works, as more often than not perfection is — in a sense — an attribute which our warm, enthusiastic artistic subjectivity bestows upon the work of art, the wish to respond most completely to the challenge of enigmatic, half told things.

That is why the "reading" of Constable's pictorial illusion made by Gombrich, the philosopher of colour, with such keen insight is all the more impressive. In his *Art and Illusion*, a study in the psychology of pictorial representation, Gombrich dwells at length — and not unsuccessfully — on a less striking picture, perhaps even rather academic at first sight, yet bearing the secret signs of a masterpiece. This is the already mentioned *Wivenhoe Park*, which marks a turning point in the work of John Constable, in which two qualities of his painting have simultaneously triumphed: the great freshness of the vision — which he acquired through a hard struggle with colour and with the laws of landscape painting at the time — and the painter's ability to scan the mysteries, the deep fluids, the hieroglyphs of nature.

Here the grass is imperceptibly "pricking" the light; the shadows of the tree-tops in the background are green, graded tones of green which absorb the solar radiations piercing through the clouds or lining them; the transparent water flecked with the shadows of clouds becomes, when contemplated for a long time a "latent nadir", the unreal realm of nature caught dreaming. All this, however, does not express a mere "Arcadian realism" but points to an extremely vivid realism stressing the peculiar features of a subtle, modern pantheism, suggesting the transience of things, universal dynamics. What Constable "really" saw at Wivenhoe Park — says Gombrich — was no doubt a house standing on the farther shores of the lake. What he had learnt to paint was a spot of colour which admitted of any interpretation, the correct one included. Ambiguity cannot be seen and therefore it stands to reason that we do not know the innumerable strange interpretations concealed beyond the clear surface of the painting. For, while we carefully examine the colours spread on the canvas in order to find an answer to the 'somewhere, over there' motif, the coherent interpretation comes of itself and illusion sets in.

In most of his canvases Constable was able to achieve a matchless brilliant freshness. We know the success the *Hay Wain* (1824) enjoyed in Paris where it attracted the enthusiastic appreciation of Charles Nodier, Delacroix or Thackeray who saw in the work of the Suffolk painter a happy moment in the history of painting, opening up new horizons for its development. It is reported that in his great admiration for *The Hay Wain* Delacroix made certain changes in his own *Massacre at Chios*. Constable's masterpiece *Salisbury Cathedral* (harmoniously blending a splendid architecture and profound lyricism), as well as the sketches made in preparation of the finished painting, the landscapes representing Suffolk, Hampstead, Weymouth, Flatford, Dedham, the series of watercolours in which he took up the same motifs over and over again and developed them from various angles, the painter's other works that have become so famous — *The White Horse*, *The Leaping Horse* and the strange *Stonehenge* — breathe the lofty poetic inspiration of the great landscape painter.

The Cornfield (1826), another masterpiece, is one of the mysterious victories of the artist always concerned with capturing all the truth in nature by means of an ever renewed language. A master of "horizontal" depths, Constable dilated as it were the space of the picture to make it comprise all the vastness of nature. There is in it a sense of space that makes the on-looker feal dizzy. But the effects the painter wants to achieve are by far subtler. Space is suggested by other means besides the usual ones. The fine granules of white scattered all over the canvas produce the unexpected effect of freshness and deep luminosity. "Constable's snow" laid on the canvas like powdery snow is only one of the devices heralding the daring innovations of the Impressionists. The concern with "light", with finding a language capable of rendering light through colour, appeared early enough with Constable. Had he not marvelled

Cloud Study with Verses from Bloomfield

at the *dewy light* he had discovered in Rubens' paintings? In fact Constable's meditations on light perfectly reflect his concern with the essence of landscape: "Perhaps what I sacrifice to light and brilliance is indeed too much. And yet they are the essence of landscape."

There is no need to stress how close such a viewpoint is to the ones professed by Monet or Pissarro. (The aesthetics of Impressionism was to learn the lesson of the Suffolk painter). Many of his great pictures — great owing to the deep feeling for nature in them — reveal the same interest in landscape; they are studies almost finished or sketches in which he raises a perpetual hymn to the beauty of nature, couched in a language similar to the poetry of a Wordsworth or Thomson. The large number of cloud studies in oil or water-colour we have already mentioned are as important for the modern expressiveness they evince. The painter who was looking into the pores of terrestrial matter with a wide open inner eye dilated with emotion, who watched the shadow pass on the lustruous leaves and the green and brown hues of the trees, the revolving spokes of the cart wheels, the spire of a cathedral and the sunbeams flashing through the dewdrops, rainbows, horses straining before the leap, barges, sailing ships, **14** walls, ploughs and county lanes, the rustic scenery with human figures in it, this painter was also able to contemplate the absolute, gazing at the sky and clouds with the élan of a visionary and the moving instinct of reverie. When looking at the sky Constable confessed with the intuition of a very modern painter: "The sky must and always shall with me be an effectual part of the composition. It will be difficult to name a class of landscape in which the sky is not the '*key note*,' the standard of '*scale*' and the chief '*organ of sentiment*.'"

We know there are data that prove beyond any doubt how much he was interested in and how eager he was to understand the problems of atmosphere.

Constable was really concerned with the physical aspect of clouds. More often than not he used to mark on the back of some cloudscapes the date, hour and direction of the wind. At the same time he was equally interested in the various ways of *rendering* the ephemeral. The method suggested by the landscape painter Cozens in his book *A New Method of Assisting the Invention in Drawing Original Composition of Landscape* (London, 1785) which had roused a wide echo at the time, was bound to interest him. He was also interested in the study by Luke Howard: "*On the Modification of Clouds*" published in London in 1820. The essential thing about these canvases — beyond any aesthetic intention or any technical or meteorological concern — is the fact that they reveal the anxiety of the artist. They are filled with a great lyrical, though not rhetorical élan, ringing with the sweet ample harmony of his heart aspiring after vast expanses. "One of these canvases," writes Mayoux, "places us right in the middle of the sky, nothing but the sky of a light diaphanous blue-grey which seems to turn into faint grey-mauve denser patches, with the exception of the upper part where they form a rather opaque background for the wonderful bluish flakes with touches of yellow coming from an invisible light which the wind carries along in long fine streaks. Broadly speaking, the canvas may be likened to *Les Nymphéas* by Monet, as absolutely pure painting."

The "clouds" are a triumph of the ineffable expressed through colour and as such there is nothing physical about them. There is no conventional scenography, no skilful arrangement, no sacrifice to spoil the poetic achievement of these constellations of vapour, of these evanescent states of dreaming matter. We can distinguish here rapture rather than science. His science lies invisible behind the touches foreshadowing Impressionism. Impetuous or resting gently in the boundless ether, fluffy or dense, whitish or dark, the clouds in the canvas to be found at the Victoria and Albert Museum make up the "Sistine" of the English romantic landscape, the same as Monet's *Nymphéas* at the Orangerie were going to be "the Sistine of Impressionism."

We assume that in the fleeting aspects of the earth, the unassuming yet passionate Constable, the artist who always avoided excess, painted with candid élan but himself.

Through the illusions, the desintegration and dreams embedded in them, through their unearthly freedom, the many canvases in which Constable painted the clouds, will perhaps always be his most genuine self-portraits.

VASILE NICOLESCU

ANTHOLOGY OF TEXTS

Few painters had Constable's power to bring the infinite facts of nature into one single pictorial idea and, with almost unconscious naturalness, to translate them into a poetic image.

ATTILIO PODESTÀ

The greatest English landscape painters: Crome, Turner, Girtin, Constable were all born between 1768 and 1776. Constable is the purest of them all, the most authentic, the artist *par excellence*. He revived the taste for the picturesque in painting and revealed the pictorial absolute in a few landscape studies. Reverting from the pictorial effect to the spiritual conditions that gave it rise, we can realize that, as compared to Wilson or Gainsborough, Constable is the painter possessing a new, far stricter moral vision. The decorative, the entertaining elements as well as the inquisitiveness peculiar to the 18th century have disappeared. Constable seems to confer upon the study of landscape the value of a national claim. The Roman plain, the Dutch beaches and the German woods are gone for ever. His landscape is an *English Landscape*. Besides freeing him from his former mannerism, moral sensitiveness brought him near to the humblest natural phenomena. All this produced a peculiar anxiety in his manner of expressing a need for vibration and life, an inclination to contrasts rather than nuances. It is true that he can err more often, but at the same time he can achieve more depth. In the struggle between neoclassics and romantics, Constable gave a strong impulse to the French romantic painters. Nevertheless he went beyond Romanticism to reach Naturalism and even surpass it.

His naturalism is candid, positive and factual, as unsentimental as painting can be; on the basis of this distinction between candid and sentimental poetry, Constable is to be included among the candid, that is the classics. However his art included landscapes only, which implies that his outlook on art was different from that of the Greeks, Latins and the Italians of the Renaissance. He started from the picturesque to reach the pictorial, grounding his conception of beauty on light and shade effects achieved through colour. He rose against those who advocated the "return to classicism", which was successful in his time, but he did it in the name of a "return to nature" which Romanticism brought along. Consequently as compared to neoclassicism Constable is a romantic.

LIONELLO VENTURI

Constable, who started from a *tavola rasa*, is the first to have organized a new space and a new form, a pictorial space and form, while Blake, who started from Michelangelo's formalism destroys space and form; Constable who looked at truth with an eye trained by the "picturesque", concerned himself with nothing but controlling the correlation, or sympathy, or equilibrium between human nature and external nature. To refer again to the distinction between Reynolds and Fuseli, Constable is an artist who possesses a rich fantasy, but a poor imagination, while Blake calculates the élan of imagination with an absolute dearth of fantasy.

GIULIO CARLO ARGAN

When *The Haywain* was exhibited in Paris in 1824 it caused a sensation. Admired by Delacroix and Corot (who were both influenced by him), Constable was thenceforward to enjoy a continuously high reputation in nineteenth-century France. And yet the English public took little account of him until long after his death. Ironically, he is now regarded as in many ways the most 'national' of English artists — certainly the supreme painter of the English scene. Unlike his great contemporary, Turner, he never travelled abroad, but directed all his efforts to recording the unemphatic outlines, the changing weather and light, the towering cloudscapes of pastoral England — above all, of his native Suffolk. Combining the lessons that he had learned from the seventeenth-century Dutch school with his own remarkable gifts and his intense regional feeling, he extended the whole realm of landscape painting and thus made an immensely important contribution to the art of the world.

GIUSEPPE GATT

His sense of the changing light, of the shadows cast by the clouds in a vast windswept sky, must have had its roots both in Ruisdael's landscapes and in his own observations. For Constable, like any innovator, carefully studied the past. He had the gift, which only great artists possess, to grasp the manner of painting apparently alien to him and to extract from it the almost fertile elements. He could assimilate without imitating. His letters prove he understood Titian, Claude Lorrain, Wilson and Gaspard Poussin; towards the end of his life he gave up any commission in order to make copies after some pictures by Poussin or Claude Lorrain. In a famous passage Leslie [1] wrote that as a young boy Constable was introduced to Sir George Beaumont who showed him his favourite picture, *"The Expulsion of Hagar"* by Claude Lorrain, today at the National Gallery. Leslie tells us that the sight of that remarkable work was an important moment in Constable's life. This hardly conscious reminiscence can be felt in *Dedham Vale* (1802), the first dated oil painting in which Constable is himself indeed. And the fact that he used the same composition in 1828 too, in a painting today at the National Gallery of Scotland, shows how deeply imprinted it was in his memory. At the time Constable was very far from Claude Lorrain. The background of his picture contains many details, the result of direct observation, which Claude Lorrain could not have added to his idealized vision. However, it is worth dwelling on the origin of the composition, for it is a fact that deep understanding of the traditions of European landscape painting was one of the reasons that go to explain why Constable was able to present such a large number of aspects he noticed quite normally without becoming as painfully banal as some later realistic painters.

Another reason is the importance he attached, in his own words, to the "chiaroscuro of nature". The phrase occurs over and over again in his letters and the context clearly shows that he used it to describe two different effects. First he meant the brilliance of light, the "morning dew, the light breeze, bloom, freshness . . . no one of which . . . has yet been perfected on the canvas of any painter in this world." As a rule this aspect of his work is considered the most original; the technique he used to obtain it — distinct touches, tiny spots of a pure white laid with the knife — exerted a decisive influence on French painting. However, what Constable called the "chiaroscuro of nature" was also the dramatic play of light and shade that should underlie any landscape composition and show the dominant feature of the sentiment with which the scene was painted. Here is what he wrote about Lee — a fashionable landscape painter: "I had never believed that his paintings were so bad. They do nothing but imitate nature, but this imitation is one of the coldest and meanest possible. Everything is completely devoid of feeling." It is this very sense of the dramatic unity of nature and his sensitive response to the freshness of nature that distinguishes Constable from his contemporaries. He accepted the fundamental truth that art should be based on one single dominant idea and that an artist's touchstone is his ability to materialize this idea, to enrich and develop it, yet never to lose sight of it or introduce accidental elements — no matter how luring — which, in the last resort, are not subjected to the initial basic conception. It is comparatively easy to reach such an aim in the classical landscape painting, in which one could resort to ideal forms in order to prevent the multiplication of details which turn the attention away from the idea pursued. This, however, is very difficult to achieve in the naturalistic landscape Constable discovered, for, here, the impressions made by real objects are the essential starting point, and the means of simplification — we have to admit it — were not prepared in advance by the style and taste of several generations. Perhaps no other painter (Rubens excepted) managed, as Constable did, to subordinate the numberless visual data of a landscape to one single pictorial idea. The painters who came later killed the idea by enriching it or rendered only the first impression, without building anything on it. The latter of these devices shortens the duration in time of the landscape and restricts the sense of the permanence of objects, though it produced some of the finest specimens in 19th century painting.

after KENNETH CLARK

---

[1] Charles Robert Leslie (1794—1858), English anecdotal painter and art professor, the author of a "Life of Constable".

Constable has left us a full repertory of his impressions in the form of sketches in oil which today are the part of his work we admire most. But the struggle was already beginning for him — as he could well realize — when these first impressions were to be changed into large size canvases.

We possess material evidence about each stage of this laborious process for several compositions: the first small oil studies which establish the theme of the painting in relation to light and shade, the pencil studies in which forms begin to take shape, detailed drawings from nature, larger studies in oil. It was only later that Constable started painting the six-footer. But the picture he made was not the one he was to exhibit. It would have been too painful for him to pass without any transition from his own way of feeling — i.e. from impression expressed by means of colour — to the conventional concept of the "finite" — i.e. to an accumulation of concepts described separately. First of all he feels the need to paint a large canvas in his own language. This is the origin of the sketches as large as the painting itself which, in fact, are Constable's finest achievements. Whether he viewed them in the same light is hard to say. He may as well have considered them just simple preparations for the pictures that were to be exhibited later and it is certain that he set great store by the various additional elements which a greater precision made him introduce into the finished painting.

We knew it not only from his letters but also from some smaller pictures such as *Willows by the River Bank* and *Trees at Hampstead: The Path to the Church* which evince his total acceptance of all the elements of vision encountered in art. It is quite significant that the former of these two paintings was not accepted by the Royal Academy in the year when they accepted *The Hay Wain*, the reaction was allegedly a too flat rendering of a given motif. Of all Constable's works, this painting would have had the chance of being accepted over the last fifty years, while *Hadleigh Castle* would have probably been rejected.

Of the great paintings by Constable, *The Hay Wain* comes closer to his general vision. His principal motif has been a source of inspiration for thousands of calendars; yet, in my opinion, the painting has outlived this crushing popularity remaining to this day, a moving expression of serenity and optimism. In some cases nature was able to breathe life into so many commonplace details; such was for instance *The Cornfield* which after his death was selected to represent him at the National Gallery. But Constable was boring only in his finished pictures. In his sketches, his impressions are powerful enough to save these works from triteness. In the sketch (as large as the picture) he made for *The Hay Wain*, emotion drove him towards a freer, more pictorial treatment which, in its turn, changed his vision. And in his most important works naturalism becomes loftier owing to his belief that, as nature is the clearest expression of God's will, landscape painting, viewed in the humble spirit of respect for truth, can be a means of conveying moral ideas.

after KENNETH CLARK

Before Constable, the sensorial data through which man was able to perceive the universe were only visual. The world was like a show, natural or arranged, function of the painters, but always felt to be an "external world", an environment designed for other kingdoms, different from the one where man was the ruler, and perceived by him — when he realized there were links between them — as a mere setting, the "theatre" in which he carried on his activity.

Constable suddenly plunges us into the substance of the world. The earth is his great discovery. What was the earth before Constable? Hardened soil, like slabs of stone, the painters had made it represent the pedestal on which man lived, a statue or an art depending on the proportions he was granted in the world. Under this film, smooth with Poussin, hard, cracked and shrunk like the skin of an old man with Ruisdael, Constable discovered the quivering flesh of the earth. He disclosed to us the mysterious universe the autumn ploughing brought to the surface. Under the amorphous sunbaked crust, hardened in summer time, odourless and easily crushed to dust between the fingers, the ploughshare turns up a warm substance, sticking to the fingers like blood, stiffling you with its heavy scent, steaming like the entrails of a killed animal. The son of the Suffolk miller had breathed in all these intoxicating sensations. I can easily imagine him a peasant, picking up a clod of earth, touching it, breathing in its pleasant smell, feeling in its inebriating fragrance the musty smell, the nourishing substances whose germs it contains.

It is Hesiod's Gaea "with her ample bosom" who carries the universe in her womb; if we rip her open bread and wine will gush forth, the linen cloth we are clad in, the stones we build our houses with, the coal — a source of energy —, the gold, diamonds, rubies, amber and jade that adorn us.

All these, clods of earth and precious stones, are present indeed in the magnificent substance, sticky and glowing red, the earth of Constable's paintings is made of; it is the incipient substance of all substances, the clay out of which Jehova created Adam. It is so warm, so palpitating, that it seems to be fluid like matter in fusion; it is the English earth, a watery soil, a sort of intermediate state between water and firm earth, oozy, soaking wet, spongious, hardly less ductile than the muddy ocean bathing its shores, pressed under by a sky covered with dense heavy clouds, so that the three elements that make up the landscape — earth, sky and water — seem to merge into a unique substance. You must have waded through the English mud, scoured the ocean of the plains in these parts somewhere in a southern county, to be able to feel that the infinite — which other people sought in space — the serf bound to the ancient soil discovered in the earth, the primordial, inexhaustible substance, unfathomable like the ocean.

Look at the *Leaping Horse!* How difficult it is for the rider to lift this rustic horse from the mud! Will he free himself from the original clay he was made of? Rich, sticky, adhesive, tentacular, the soil Constable painted puts me in mind of the sublime words a peasant from the province of Beauce uttered once when we were out hunting. Seeing that I was so suprised that a sort of mud sole about 20 centimetres thick had stuck to my boots after I had walked some 200 metres in the field, he said: "The earth here is friendly". Yes, but isn't this earth friendly to all of us and everywhere, Gaea, the one who is a mother for us human beings? Doesn't she represent Love? What fiery pulsations of her heart make her bosom heave? It is the thrill of Eros, the brother-principle that suddenly makes substances and living beings discover their affinities and urges them to unite. In a powerful élan of brotherhood, Constable feels everything that binds his heart to the Universe, to the everlasting chain of living beings and of objects. "Painting is with me but another word for feeling," the painter used to say. He inaugurated the aesthetics of sensation. His pictures reveal saturated senses, an intoxicated heart, anxious at the thought that he will not be able to say everything that oppresses him. No other painter was to express romantic pantheism more deeply than he did.

GERMAIN BAZIN

Constable's originality is made up of all this, of his timid attempts at freeing himself from the tyranny of the Dutch painters, of Hobbema more especially — whom he was ambitious enough for a time to outrival and took a long time to forget —, of his clumsy endeavours to bring together dream and reality — for he was less skilful than Turner in this respect —, of his desire to fix movement and to breathe life into the most static objects by means of inner mobility. Constable rejuvenated painting for he made it its aim to render what is for ever young, familiar things you contemplate every day with renewed wonder for they become more and more surprising with every passing day ... He had discovered that light is not colourless, that it is not altogether transparent, that it has a *body*, and this was the cause of inexhaustible wonder. He had a peculiar way of breathing in the air, which was sensual and spiritual at one and the same time.

He had started from Nature and had reached Nature shunning the temptations of academism which were not dangerous to him for he had defended himself against their threats. His portraits sold well, his landscapes roused no interest at first, and his father the miller, considered that the profession of painter was too hazardous and that there were few prospects in it unless you were a fashionable artist such as Gainsborough and Reynolds were. When he had acquired a thorough classical knowledge, Constable turned away from the comfortable, profitable roads; he feared the facile perverse temptation of illusionism offered by the panoramas and dioramas so much prized in the London of the 1810s. He had to forget the experience acquired in the capital — except for the technical means of expression, no doubt, which his sincerity could use without lying ... — and to look at every object as if he had never seen it before. He was never in quest of the picturesque, and everything beyond measure, mountains or lakes made no impression on him, as Leslie tells us. He was a poet and a moralist. "I never saw an ugly thing in my life," he used to say; no matter the form of an object, the light, the shade and the perspective will always make it beautiful.

Any attempt at arranging or *embelishing* for the sake of an effect hurt him as if it were something dishonest, improper, impious. An artist must contemplate nature ingenuously, almost impassively, waiting for the state of grace, persuaded that in its supreme revelations nature like Isis never lifts its veil completely. This state of grace was to be begged for, wished for in a humble pious élan, for one can never do violence to beauty. "No arrogant man was ever permitted to see nature in all her beauty." This is a statement William Blake would have subscribed to himself.

It would be possible to make up a moving collection with Constable's various remarks. Though he had become rather didactical in his lectures, he gave no lessons but rather keys that unlocked the secret world of things. He does not speak for some possible disciples, he soliloquizes as if to remember some eternal truths, the secrets of age-old wisdom, the warnings he got from nature when he went for a walk, all his senses alert; for with him the sense of smell and of feeling in his palms and his fingertips were as keen and vigilant as his sight. The inexhaustible diversity of things and moments filled him with delight and surprise: "No two days are alike not even two hours; neither were there ever two leaves of a tree alike since the creation of the world." To get to know oneself, to know the real limits of one's abilities, but also to know how far one's own abilities can go, this is — in his opinion — to be great; yet, an unassuming man, Constable believed that "the great was not made for the great". Therefore great was *la maniera grande* of the Italians, of Salvator Rossa, of Poussin, of Hobbema, but when he said "my limited art can be found under each hedge-row and on every pathway" he was defining it, without claiming to do so, as a real investigation of the infinite, for indeed his art had no more limits than nature has.

The great stir caused among the French artists by the great English exhibition of 1824 at the Louvre, — whose influence was so strong that it made French Romanticism start upon a course it hesitated to engage upon, shows that Constable, who had scored the greatest success in the event was considered in France a Romantic *par excellence*. His success in France was by far greater than the one he had obtained in his own country. The English had always enjoyed a favourable reception in France where *anglomania* had become traditional; but the 1824 exhibition corresponded to profound aesthetic concerns and to some yet vague, not very precise researches; French artists regretted Constable the Romantic had not been born in Paris, and saw in his manner of painting landscapes a frank, vivid freedom, a fresh sensitiveness and emotion they had never encountered in France before...

However, Constable was too "natural" for a society of collectors and critics who still regarded the English landscape painting with an eye formed by the Dutch and French painting of the 17th century and of the Italian painters of the Baroque, (who readily dramatized things in their pictures).

On the contrary, in Constable's early landscapes one can see a feeling of truth completely devoid of any sentimental attachment; he does not dramatize nature in order to make it suited to his feelings which, in fact, are very seldom dramatic. He loves above all the peaceful and happy nature which is never complicated by the metaphysical considerations so dear to the Germans.

The painter himself becomes nature, tree and plain, changes without any effort into the very things he loves, and shuns more and more the company of men the deeper he plunges in his communion with the objects in rustic nature, acquiring new senses in order to perceive and understand them... His ample pictorial style, based on what he had become himself, on what he stood for, had already taken full shape when in 1806 he painted *Malvern Hill* (National Gallery, London) in which the ample breath of the English field is dilating as it were in the calm landscape where the art of the gardener cooperates with nature itself in the freest and happiest manner. However, he seems to be drawn more especially by the boundless expanse of sky and water the shores of the English Channel showed him, by the luminosity of the atmosphere saturated with moisture which he feels through all his pores and in which he can perceive the play of light and shade inviting him to scrutinize, spiritually and technically, what he calls the "chiaroscuro of nature". At the same time, his vision has the merits of analysis, which divides colours, — Delacroix had been greatly impressed by the fact that Constable used to say that "the superiority of the green colour of his plains resides in that it is made up of a multitude of different shades of green" — and the energy of the synthesis of chromatic energies which flourish in all the tones and all the sonorities of this orchestration of browns, greens and whites.

He aspires after the "pure perception of the natural fact", but he could not do it after the fashion of the Impressionists for there is in him — no doubt unconsciously — a religious feeling of art, a pantheistic devotion to the elements and the sky first, which is as he used to say "the keynote, the standard of scale, the chief organ of sentiment." The English landscape appears to him as a living being, immense and multiform, possessing at the same time the essential stability of rocks thrust deep into the earth and the unceasing mobility of branches, clouds and waters. He wanted to be a realist — until he was about forty — but as he became more clearly and more deeply aware of the musicality of the English countryside which he never wanted to leave, the romanticism implicitly included in the paintings he made before 1820 burst forth freely until, towards the end of his life, the tragical sentiment he had carefully kept far away from his work and from himself eventually conquered him. In 1830 he painted *The Dell in Helmingham Park* (Tate Gallery) which is a composition of his anxiety and the presentiment of the abyss he came close to at times. Mysterious and maleficent, the large dusky hole gaping under the oak-trees, which the still waters in the dell make deeper, points to the new direction Constable's sensitiveness and art were to take. The control he exerted over his sentiments forbidding him to feel passions other than those nature herself did, was curbed by this anxiety which irrupts now, more manifest even in *Hadleigh Castle* (National Gallery, London, 1829) in which the English ruins recall a Rhenish burgh and where the painter almost joins the German Romanticism by the spirit animating the picture more than by the very original technique.

"Hadleigh Castle", which was more seriously misjudged by English connoisseurs than any other of Constable's paintings, moves us deeply as it is the romantic testament of an artist who now lets crumble all the barriers which formerly arrested the invasion of the pathetic into his art. The long, clayey plain, the sea that seems to thicken its waves, with the silt of the depths, the ravens flying low, the dull heavy sky, envelop the crumbling tower in an almost supernatural atmosphere, so oppressive as to produce anxiety. This painting is a challenge to the English connoisseurs, to nature, a reappearance of the anxiety and fear the apparent innocence of nature had kept hidden from him. Nature now offers him a mirror in which he can see nothing but his own troubled conscience despite the brilliant outbursts of youth and genius which still uplifted him so frequently, of which his watercolours are the best example *(Old Sarum*, Victoria and Albert Museum, 1834). With *Hadleigh Castle* John Constable's romanticism reached a climax he could never surpass: it is one of the highest English Romanticism was able to attain . . .

MARCEL BRION

Because during the most creative years of his career, from 1819 to 1825, he had striven to bring painting on to a plane of greater sincerity, he could no longer attain grandeur in the works which receive the greatest prestige. A limbo awaits him where his shade walks, suspended between the ancient and the modern, just as the figures in Dante's limbo, "neither sad nor joyful." He was not so modern as to cause scandal; he was modern enough to please only a few. He was dogged by the shadow of moderate success, perhaps a greater torment than the scorn and total failure which afflicted his greatest followers, the impressionists. He was always under the impression that he had not had enough out of life.

ARCANGELI

The greatest thing the English landscape was able to achieve with Old Crome, Cotman, Bonington and Constable more especially, was to supply Delacroix with some of the technical elements of lyricism which were to breathe life into French painting for eighty years running and which is still alive. When Delacroix saw Constable's landscapes the year he was painting his *Massacre at Chios,* he changed his vast canvas in four days only. He discovered in them a principle, the division of colours, almost instinctively achieved by Veronese, Vermeer de Delft and Chardin, whose productivity, however, Constable was deliberately demonstrating with the rigour and scrupulousness of the English. When closely examined, one can see red tones, orange, green, blue and yellow, a jumble of juxtaposed colours, apparently bearing no relation whatever to the distant colouring they claim to imitate from nature and the clear form they want to suggest. From a distance, we can see the vast sky, pale blue and limpid, where pearly clouds are sailing like ships, the veil of filmy water always floating, quivering as it were over the plain, the blue mists that grow thicker as they lose themselves in the distance. Here is the boundless plain, so lush, so green in England after the rain that it seems to be spreading over a giant palette thick with dewdrops. Everything — the thick Sward, the deep mass of the oak-trees, the white and red houses peeping out of the green coppices, the azure and silver sky, the flowers covered with dewdrops — everything is shining and quivering and sparkling like a world coming to life in its freshest and most transparent hour. "I am the resurrection and life," the rustic plains told Constable. His heart plunged into them like a woman's most beautiful body into water.

When Constable achieved such transparency he came closest to great painting, and he was perhaps a greater painter when he used watercolour than when he tried to render by means of oil — so generously used by Reynolds and his group — the moist and irridiscent brilliancy of the English landscape. Watercolour, by its lack of thickness, its liquid freshness, its inability to render too subtle nuances, is the medium best suited to the English. Constable owes it his most limpid watercolours.

ELIE FAURE

To invariably describe *its own self* is the most characteristic feature of the spirit. It is a pattern in a state of perpetual flow, of ceaseless creation and destruction, and its activity in this connection is an artistic one. The same as the artist, the spirit influences nature. That is what it does with everything physical reality offers so carelessly and bountifully and, starting from these premises, it never ceases its processing activity. The spirit tries to appropriate them, to breathe life into them, to give them *shape*. Our fundamental psychological activity consists in an integrating process, the search of an equilibrium between the spirit, the mind and the external world. Constable's durable and lucid existence is this very equilibrium, the harmonious moment of integration.

after HERBERT READ

In Constable's opinion two were the things that had to be avoided: absurd imitation and *bravura*, trying to do something that transcends the truth. The main thing is to grasp the facts of nature. We do not really see anything unless we understand. But to understand nature is not easy at all. "The landscape painter must walk in the fields with a humble mind." He must not study nature with the same humble attitude but with the seriousness and zeal of the scientist. The art of reading nature is something one must learn the same as the art of reading the Egyptian hieroglyphs. No doubt the painter must be compared with a poet of nature and it is strange indeed that the extraordinary parallelism between Constable and Wordsworth is not emphasized more often. The two were almost contemporary and what each created in his own art is almost the same thing. Both cleansed their art of the derived "eclectic" mannerisms, both returned to the facts of nature and created their art by intuiting them, and both produced a revolution in their respective domains. It happens that both represent the spirit of the English landscape with an intensity never matched before and I find it impossible to imagine a book that should be more illustrative of English beauty than a collection of Wordsworth's poems illustrated by a few paintings by Constable.

after HERBERT READ

The Valley Farm is the summation of a lifetime's work and a sinister object it is. Constable's concern with the subject goes back to the turn of the century. And the picture bears all the marks of obsession. Constable describes himself in the studio at night — 'Oiling out, making out, polishing, scraping, etc.' He painted, rubbed down, and painted again, literally torturing the picture surface. Of colour, so long regarded by Constable as his special strength, there is scarcely a trace (what would he have said now to Sir George's question, where do you put your brown tree?). Willy Lott's Cottage was to him the emblem of the natural life, of man and nature in concord. But the idyll is fading. That silent couple in the boat going nowhere, cows half sunk in stagnant water, the black beggar at the gate — they are creatures in a bad, bad dream.

CONAL SHIELDS and LESLIE PARRIS

He wanted nothing but the truth ... Constable had no wish to shock people by daring innovations. All he wanted was to be faithful to his own conceptions ... But however great and deserved was the popular success which some of these Romantic painters achieved in their day, we believe today that those who followed Constable's path and tried to explore the visible world rather than to conjure up poetic moods achieved something of more lasting importance.

E. H. GOMBRICH

Constable's own evolution was more complex and unsettled than some of the exhibition pieces painted in his forties suggest. The sketches, which were hardly known for fifty years after his death in 1837, tell another, private story in which the man who wrote that "painting is with me but another word for feeling" is to our eyes more clearly recognizable.

22

In them his impulsive brush is set free: its movement sweeps the color like a wind. In the sketches Constable is discovered, at one with the poets of his time, "identifying his own feelings with external nature."

Visual realism showed Constable a way to the whole sense and sentiment of landscapes, to "the sound of water escaping from milldams, etc., willows, old rotten planks, slimy posts, and brickwood, I love such things." Light led him, not to Impressionism but to the conversion, of all luminous phenomena into the material of emotional expression (for which he borrowed the word *chiaroscuro*) — to "dews, breezes, bloom, and freshness, not one of which has yet been perfected on the canvas of any painter in the world."

LAWRENCE GOWING

Constable says that the superiority of the green colour of his meadows resides in the fact that he made it out of a multitude of different shades of green. The lack of intensity and life we perceive in the green colour most of the landscape painters use can be ascribed to the fact that they use a uniform tone. What he says about the green colour of the meadows holds good for every other tone.

EUGÈNE DELACROIX

Thick brush-strokes alternate with areas treated in the same way as watercolours. Colours vary from dry, thinly-applied tones to brilliant, heavy-textured patches, from an all-enveloping silvery glow to a sudden frenzy of wild emotion. Light is the unifying factor, bringing animation and vigour.

GRAHAM REYNOLDS

After 1830 Constable was mainly concerned to bring his paintings to a greater degree of 'finish': his work seemed to be a long meditation on the pictorial themes of his lifetime. Those were the themes which were essential features in the development of European art and had enabled Constable — 'the first modern painter' — to anticipate by half a century the discovery of impressionism.

GIUSEPPE GATT

In point of technique Constable is the first definitely "modern" painter. His manner of painting is already that of the Barbizon painters and of the early impressionists: he is far removed from the severe execution of the classics as well as from Gainsborough's skilful, ineffable execution. His painting is rich in substance like solid matter, rapid but precise and convincing, a painting in which each touch is selected and decided upon unfalteringly, with extraordinary exact precision. No matter the poetic feeling animating him, each of his paintings is a perfect product in which the finest possible quality is achieved without any obvious effort, without even the impulse of an emotional outburst, of an emotional agitation, according to a perfect method or device. Of course there is no point in seeking any analogy with the productive technique of English industry about to be born: such an affinity — to resort to some scientific or pseudo-scientific expedient — could be sooner noticed with Turner who is an *avant-garde* painter, as we might say today and — as such — antiacademic and antitradionalist, but in fact very much taken up with tradition. In exchange, Constable is modern without being modernistic, and less than ever a revolutionary: he is a producer of good and excellent painting, who does not consider technique to be an ideal or a problem, but has a perfect command of it, and who has developed the cult of, though not yet the fetishism for, the quality of a product. There is no longer anything of the artisan in his painting: of course his technique has nothing mechanical about it; yet, independent and well-achieved as it is, it corresponds to the new production techniques. As pure, genuine painting, it claims to be as legitimate and positive as science or politics; and it is never, not even for a moment, desertion or sentimental escapism.

The taste for the "sublime" is obviously on the wane: and one of the causes was no doubt the imposing character and vivacity of Constable's manner of painting. In spite of all his efforts to be "modern", Turner is considered today as one of the great representatives of an outdated taste, while Constable roused the most vivid interest by the clear "figurative" quality of his work as solid and brilliant as Turner's was evanescent and ineffable.

The competition which from now on becomes almost dramatic left its deep imprint upon the style of the two painters. The more stubbornly Constable refused any theoretical, literary or poetic premise and followed his painter's sure instinct and his extraordinary ability to surprise and fix the presence of light in the most humble object — on a thatched roof, in

23

the reflection of a pool or in the blade of moist grass —, the more Turner seems to have turned to the rendering of light as a pure cosmic entity, light-space, disregarding those things in which light tangibly manifests itself. The more Constable tried to discover the familiar trait present in every object, to glorify the tiniest detail by means of light, the more Turner seems to have sought refuge in Reynold's famous principle of "generalization", even if beyond the "type" he sought a new universality, the "modern sublime", in the diffused spatial luminosity.

GIULIO CARLO ARGAN

What has Constable's example become for French Art? The elegiac character of his works did not surprise the painters who still took into account the vigorous tradition of Poussin, were contemporary with the capricious works of Théodore Rousseau and were soon to witness the appearance of Corot and his elegiac sentimental period. The same holds good for the cult of nature so obvious in the works of Constable. The authors of the "vues pitoresques" overemphasized these sentiments. And yet, though the dialogue with nature was not a discovery in itself, the way in which it was carried on is no doubt an important achievement of the English artist. His new palette played also an important role.

Freeing himself from the brown tones prevailing at the time, renouncing the dark lines, Constable acquired the purity of the palette which is the main charm of the classic painting *Weymouth Bay* (1816—1817) and *Salisbury Cathedral* (about 1829). It gave food for thought even to the famous colourist Delacroix was.

ALEKSANDER WOJCIECHOWSKI

So it was moral seriousness and not naturalistic precision that made Constable state the day and hour of his landscape surpassing not only romanticism but also realism and reaching thus an impressionist programme. "The world is wide," he used to say, "no two days are alike, not even two hours; neither were there ever two leaves of a tree alike since the creation of the world; and the genuine productions of art, like those of nature, are all distinct from each other." From the individual character of nature's creations Constable rises to the individuality of artistic creations. He holds that any original painting is an independent study indeed, governed by its own laws, so that what is true in one of them is altogether erroneous when referred to another.

Some ideal consequences arise from this outlook which individualizes nature and the work of art. First of all he renounced panoramic effects. In order to individualize he had to restrict the motif to a fragment of nature. This implied the idea that any tiny fragment of nature contains in it universal beauty, the same as any genuine painting contains universal art.

Another idea implied here: each corner of nature possesses a multiple physiognomy; therefore a variation of natural light is enough to turn any motif in a landscape into a new artistic one. On the other hand, in order to feel at one with nature, to take part in the complex life of nature itself, Constable avoids the exceptional effects the Romantics were so fond of. Moreover he voiced his protest against the "prodigious, astonishing" phenomena. He painted neither autumn nor winter. He preferred spring and painted the prolonged spring summer is in England.

With his basically simple manner of feeling and his moral seriousness, Constable wanted to lend durability and calm to those fleeting evanescent appearances. And he writes: "I wish my painting could render light, dew, the blowing wind, the blooming flowers, freshness, nothing that any painter has represented so far." This is Constable's romanticism: the visual expression of the intangible. Yet, while looking at some of his canvases who would dare to say he has not succeeded? This is a typical instance of the miracle art performs.

LIONELLO VENTURI

He devised a powerful, direct technique: bright colours juxtaposed in thin touches, or — when he considers it suitable and more and more in his last canvases — in patches which the knife spread on the canvas; and especially a technique his friends called "Constable's snow", tiny white dots designed to render the infinite scintillation of light on the moist surface.

This simple technique, this proud desire of being all alone in front of nature is the most invaluable legacy he left modern art; first to the painters of Fontainebleau, then to the Impressionists.

AURÉLIEN DIGEON

CHRONOLOGY
AND CONCORDANCES

1768   *The English landscape painter Richard Wilson exhibits his "Lake Nemi with Two Monks", which seems to herald Constable's colour modulation. J. J. Mayoux holds that his landscapes are the finest ever painted before Constable, though they possess none of the brilliant eloquence of Gainsborough's works. In fact, Constable himself was to say about Wilson, in 1823, that he remembered nothing else other than Wilson's great landscape, solemn and bright, warm and fresh at the same time. Wilson entered the noble army of martyrs, he showed the world what existed in nature and what had not been seen yet.*
Joseph Wright of Derby, a visionary landscape painter of great emotional power, paints the famous canvas Experiment with a Pneumatic Bell.
Birth of the landscape painter John Crome — Old Crome.

1770   *Birth of William Wordsworth.*

1772   *Birth of Samuel Taylor Coleridge.*

1775   *Birth of Thomas Girtin, one of the most fascinating English landscape painters.*
Birth of Joseph Mallord Turner — a towering personality of English and world painting — in Covent Garden.

1776   Birth of John Constable, son of a miller, on June 11, in the village of East Bergholt, Suffolk, a county with fresh, radiant landscapes, shady canals and rivers, water and wind mills.

1785   *The landscape painter Cozens, after having come to public notice thanks to the daring visions in his pictures, also famous for his studies on the various manners of interpreting the sky and the trees by means of colour, publishes — starting with an idea of Leonardo da Vinci — his work* A New Method of Assisting the Invention in Drawing Original Compositions of Landscape.
A subtle innovator of water-colour techniques, of the "ink-blot" technique particularly, Cozens greatly enriched the science of landscape painting, even if he is sometimes rhetorical and fantastic. Possessing great sensitiveness, Cozens is one of the first painters to consider landscape a spiritual mood too.

1788   *Birth of Lord Byron.*
Death of Thomas Gainsborough.
Death of John Robert Cozens.

1789   *William Blake brings out his volume of verse* Songs of Innocence.

1790   *Immanuel Kant writes his* Critique of Judgement.

1792   *Birth of Percy Bysshe Shelley.*

1795   In London, Constable takes engraving lessons with John Thomas Smith.

       Birth of John Keats.

1797   *Publication of* The Ancient Mariner *and* Kubla Khan *by Coleridge.*

       The painter returns to Bergholt and works as a miller together with his father.

1798   *Birth of Delacroix.*

1799   Goes on a new trip to London during which, following a letter of recommendation by Joseph Farington — a pupil of Richard Wilson — he is admitted to the Royal Academy as a student.

       Fuseli starts his lectures at the Royal Academy.
Turner paints the watercolour Norham Castle.
Birth of Honoré de Balzac.
Laplace publishes his Mécanique céleste.

1800   *F.W.J. Shelling publishes* The System of Transcendental Idealism.

1801   Visits Derbyshire where he paints watercolours, as was the custom at the time. *Valley Scene with Trees* dates from the period.

1802   Takes part for the first time in the Summer Salon opened at the Royal Academy. Wishing to give his entire attention to a personal sincere expression, a convinced naturalist, on the other hand rather disappointed with his pictorial endeavours, Constable confesses: "I shall return to Bergholt, where I shall endeavour to get a pure and unaffected manner of representing the scenes that may employ me. There is room enough for a natural painter. The great vice of the present day is *bravura*, an attempt to do something beyond truth."
Paints *Dedham Vale*, a subject that will always arrest his attention.

Turner paints The Tenth Calamity of Egypt.
Birth of Victor Hugo.

1803   Paints *Boats on the Orwell* and *Stream, Trees and Meadows*.

Fuseli finishes his hallucinating composition Blinded Polyphemus.

1804   Back to Suffolk, paints the portraits for which he was commissioned by the residents.

1805   *Birth of Samuel Palmer who was to paint his fine pictures* Bright Cloud *and* The Magic Apple Tree.

1806   Travels to the Lake District whence he returns with some important watercolours, *Borrowdale* among others.
Executes many copies after paintings by Reynolds and Hopner for Lord Dysart.

Hegel completes his work Phenomenology of the Spirit.

1806—1809 Executes *Head of a Girl*, the moving portrait of his younger sister.
Paints *Shipping in the Orwell, near Ipswich*. Lucas was to reproduce in 1838 a sketch of this work with the title *View over the Orwell, near Ipswich*.

1808   Struggling against the conventional language of painting, the same as Wordsworth did, advocating a return to naturalness and sincerity in poetic diction, the painter becomes himself again in *View at Epsom*.

1809   Achieves *Malvern Hall*, a painting whose virtues demonstrate that the artist is able to create a universe of his own, with a sure instinct and simplicity.

1811   Executes several oils on canvas: *Flatford Mill from a Lock on the Stour, A Village Fair, East Bergholt, Morning in Dedham Vale*. Falls in love with Maria Bricknell, grand daughter of the Rector of East Bergholt, and proposes to her. His wish was to come true only six years later.

Goya completes his famous series of engravings Los Desastres de la Guerra.

1812   As they are spiritually alike, the painter's friendship with John Fisher, Archdeacon of Salisbury, also stimulated his creative enthusiasm, in a very serious dialogue on art. Paints *Landscape with a Double Rainbow*.

Byron writes Childe Harold.

1814   Executes several oil paintings on canvas, cardboard or paper: *Spring, East Bergholt Common, Flowers in a Glass Vase, Study of Flowers, Study of Two Ploughs, Study of Cart and Horses, The Mill Stream*.

1816   The artist's marriage. It is during this period that he paints his most luminous landscapes. Paints, among others, *Wheatfield with Figures, Weymouth Bay, Willy Lott's House, Wivenhoe Park*.

1817   Still more significant are *A Cottage in a Cornfield* and *Flatford Mill on the Stour*.

1819   Elected corresponding member to the Royal Academy.
Executes *Hampstead Heath*.
The White Horse and *The Opening of Waterloo Bridge* belong to the same period.

1820   *Stratford Mill.*
Discovers Luke Howard's work *On the Modification of Clouds*.
Makes a first study of Salisbury Cathedral — an echo of the powerful impression the cathedral made on him in 1811 when he saw it for the first time. Though fresh, direct, inspired, the painting is far removed from the masterpiece he achieved in 1823.

1821   Sends in for exhibition *The Hay Wain* which greatly impresses Charles Nodier, then on a visit to London.
Completes *Dedham Mill* and *Buildings on Rising Ground near Hampstead, Study of Trees, Study for The Hay Wain* and *Study of Sky and Trees*.

Géricault's The Raft of Medusa *is exhibited in London.*

1822   *Death of Percy Byshe Shelley.*

Paints *View over the Stour*.

Birth of Baudelaire and Dostoievski.
Champollion deciphers The Rosetta Stone.

1823   Paints the first version of *Salisbury Cathedral from the Bishop's Ground* and *Evening in Hampstead*.

1824   Is prevailed upon to participate in the Paris Salon where he sends in to be exhibited his already famous *Hay Wain*, a *View from the Stour* and a small *Yarmouth*. Enjoys a huge success. Paints *Brighton Beach, 17 July 1824* and *Beach Scene with Fishing Boats*. Begins to work on *Marine Study with Rain Clouds*.

Death of Lord Byron.

1825   Exhibits *The Leaping Horse*.

1826   Paints *The Cornfield* and *The Country Road*. Starts working *Dedham Mill*.

William Blake brings out his illustrations for Dante's Divine Comedy.

1827   *Death of William Blake.*
Publication of Cromwell *by Victor Hugo.*

1828   Death of the painter's wife.

Death of Bonington.

Sends in for exhibition *Dedham Mill* **which** he had started executing two years before, and completes *Dedham Vale*.

1829   Is elected member to the Royal Academy.
Paints *Water Meadows near Salisbury* and *Hadley Castle* which some critics consider to be "the most naturally tragic."

1830   The English Landscape, *a series of mezzotints after Constable's composition, executed by David Lucas is issued with the intention of rivalling Turner's* Liber Studiorum.

Executes *View on the Stour: Dedham Church in the Distance* in pencil and sepia gouache.

Turner paints one of his masterpieces, Interior at Petworth.
Birth of Camille Pissarro.
Delacroix exhibits Freedom Guiding the People.

1832   *Birth of Edouard Manet.*

1834   *Birth of J.A.McNeill Whistler.*
Rude completes his famous bas-relief La Marseillaise.

1835   Constable lectures on the art of landscape painting at the Royal Institute in London and at the Royal Academy.
Composes the watercolour *Stonehenge*.

1836   Paints *The Cenotaph of Cole Orton, in Memory of Sir Joshua Reynolds* a late work in which romantic mannerist elements as well as a certain academism are triumphant.

Emerson publishes Nature.

1837   Death of the painter on 31 March, at the age of 61.

1839   *Birth of Paul Cézanne and Alfred Sisley.*

1840   *Birth of Claude Monet* (14 November).

SELECTIVE BIBLIOGRAPHY

F. E. HALLIDAY, *An Illustrated Cultural History of England*, Thames and Hudson, London, 1972.

KENNETH CLARK, *The Romantic Rebellion*, John Murray, London 1973.

LAWRENCE GOWING, *Constable*, Harry N. Abrams Publishers, Inc., New York

J. J. MAYOUX, *La peinture anglaise*, A. Colin, Paris, 1969.

ALEKSANDER WOJCIECHOWSKI, *Arta peisajului* (Landscape and Art), (Romanian edition), Meridiane Publishing House, Bucharest, 1974.

ELIE FAURE, *Histoire de l'art. L'Art moderne*, I, Le Livre de Poche, Paris, 1972.

LOUIS HEWES, *Constable's Sky Sketches*, "Journal of the Warburg and Courtauld Institute", Vol. XXX, London, 1969.

HUBERT DAMISH, *Théorie du nuage*, Editions du Seuil, Paris, 1972.

GIUSEPPE GATT, *Constable*, Thames and Hudson, London, 1974.

CONAL SHIELDS and LESLIE PARRIS, *John Constable*, Tate Gallery, London, 1973.

LESLIE PARRIS, IAN FLEMING WILLIAMS, *Constable. Paintings, Watercolours and Drawings*, The Tate Gallery, London, 1976.

PAUL SIGNAC, *D'Eugène Delacroix au néo-impressionisme*, Introduction et notes par Françoise Cachin, Hermann, 1964, Coll. Miroirs de l'Art, 1971.

GERMAIN BAZIN, *Histoire de l'avant-garde en peinture du XIIIe au XXe siècle*, Hachette, Paris, 1969.

GIULIO CARLO ARGAN, *Del Bramante al Canova*, Bulzoni Editore, 1970.

AURÉLIEN DIGEON, *L'École anglaise de peinture*, Editions Pierre Tisné, Paris.

MAURICE SERULLAZ, *L'Impressionisme*, P.U.F., Paris, 1972.

GEORGE OPRESCU, *Considerații asupra artei moderne* (Notes on Modern Art), Meridiane Publishing House, Bucharest, 1969.

MAURICE GROSSER, *L'Oeil du peintre*, Marabout Université, Verviers, 1955.

HANS l.c. JAFFE, *Histoire générale de la peinture, XIXe et XXe siècles*, Flammarion, Paris, 1968.

LIONELLO VENTURI, *Modern European Art*, Thames and Hudson, London, 1972.

URSULA HOFF, *The National Gallery of Victoria*, Thames and Hudson, London, 1973.

WILLIAM GAUNT, *A Concise History of English Painting*, Thames and Hudson, London, 1976.

WILLIAM GAUNT, *Modern Art. From Impressionism to the Present Day*, Frederick Warne & Co., Ltd. London, 1964.

JEAN CLAY, *L'Impressionisme*, Hachette, Paris, 1971.

PHEOBE POOL, *Impressionism*, Thames and Hudson, London, 1967.

RENÉ HUYGHE, *Sens et destin de l'art*, Flammarion, Paris, 1967.

JOHN WALKER, *National Gallery, Washington*, Editions Aimery Somogy, Paris, 1967.

E. H. GOMBRICH, *Story of Art*, Phaidon Press, Ltd., London, 1950.

E. H. GOMBRICH, *Art and Illusion*, Phaidon Press Ltd., London, 1968.

x x x *Dictionnaire universel de l'art et des artistes*, Fernand Hazan, Paris, 1967.

x x x *Histoire illustrée de la peinture. De l'art rupestre à l'art abstrait*, Fernand Hazan, 1971.

HERBERT READ, *The Meaning of Art*, Pitman, New York, 1951.

HERBERT READ, *The Philosophy of Modern Art*, Faber and Faber, London, 1969.

KENNETH CLARK, *Landscape into Art*, John Murray, London, 1952.

PHILIP HENDY, *Trésors de la peinture à la National Gallery London*, Editions Aimery Somogy, Paris, 1960.

JOHN ROTHENSTEIN, *La Tate Gallery Londres*, Editions Aimery Somogy, Paris, 1963.

LIST OF REPRODUCTIONS

In the text:

WINDMILL ON EAST BERGHOLT HEATH
1792
Incised wood
The Victor Batte-Lay Trust, The Minories, Colchester

THE ARTIST'S CHILDREN PLAYING THE COACH DRIVER
Pen an ink and watercolour
Private Collection

STUDY OF PLANTS
1828
Oil on canvas
British Museum, London

SKY STUDY
c. 1819
Crayons on blue paper
A. L. Gordon Collection

CLOUD STUDY WITH VERSES FROM BLOOMFIELD
1817
Ink, on paper watermarked 1817
Tate Gallery, London

Plates

1. THE VALLEY OF THE STOUR
   1805
   Pencil and watercolour
   Private collection
2. GIRL AND DOG IN A LANDSCAPE
   c. 1789
   Watercolour and pencil
   Dr. Roy Price Collection
3. STUDY FOR "THE BRIDGES FAMILY"
   1804 Pencil
   Denys Oppé Collection
4. ABRAM CONSTABLE
   Oil on Canvas
   Ipswich Borough Council
5. A COUNTRY LANE
   c. 1809—1814
   Oil on paper
   Tate Gallery, London

6. THE GAMEKEEPER'S HUT
   1816
   Pencil
   Royal Institution of Cornwall, Truro
7. FLATFORD MILL FROM A LOCK ON THE STOUR
   c. 1811
   Oil on canvas
   Victoria and Albert Museum, London
8. VIEW AT EPSOM
   c. 1809
   Oil on millboard
   Tate Gallery, London
9. BARGES ON THE STOUR, WITH DEDHAM CHURCH IN THE DISTANCE
   c. 1811
   Oil on paper laid on canvas
   Victoria and Albert Museum, London
10. PORTRAIT OF THE REV. J. FISHER
    exhibited in 1817
    Oil on canvas
    Fitzwilliam Museum, Cambridge
11. DEDHAM VALLEY WITH PLOUGHMAN
    c. 1815
    Oil on canvas
    Paul Mellon Collection
12. CHILD FROM SUFFOLK: SKETCH FOR "THE VALLEY FARM"
    Pencil and watercolour
    Victoria and Albert Museum, London
13. TWO GLEANERS
    c. 1815
    Pencil
    Musée du Louvre, Paris
14. THE MILL STREAM
    1813—1814
    Oil on cardboard
    Tate Gallery, London
15. THE MILL STREAM
    Exhibited in 1814
    Oil on canvas
    Christchurch Mansion, Ipswich
16. DEDHAM LOCK AND MILL
    1820
    Oil on canvas
    Victoria and Albert Museum, London

17. A HAYFIELD NEAR EAST
BERGHOLT AT SUNSET
1812
Oil on paper
Victoria and Albert Museum, London

18. SELF-PORTRAIT
1800
Pencil and watercolour on paper
National Portrait Gallery, London

19. WIVENHOE PARK, ESSEX
Exhibited in 1817
Oil on canvas
National Gallery of Art, Washington
D.C.

20. BOAT-BUILDING NEAR FLATFORD
MILL
1815
Oil on canvas
Victoria and Albert Museum, London

21. WEYMOUTH BAY
c. 1817
Oil on canvas
National Gallery, London

22. MARIA BICKNELL
1816
Oil on canvas
Tate Gallery, London

23. SELF-PORTRAIT
1806
Pencil on paper
J. H. Constable Collection

24. DEDHAM LOCK AND MILL
1810—1815
Oil on canvas
Victoria and Albert Museum, London

25. SALISBURY   CATHEDRAL   FROM
THE RIVER
1820
Oil on canvas
London, National Gallery,

26. FLATFORD MILL ON THE RIVER
STOUR
1817
Oil on canvas
London, Tate Gallery,

27. LANDSCAPE WITH TREES AND
COTTAGES UNDER A LOWERING
SKY
1812
Oil on canvas laid on millboard
Victoria and Albert Museum, London

28. STUDY OF CUMULUS   CLOUDS
1822
Oil on paper on panel
Paul Mellon Collection

29. CLOUD   STUDY: HORIZON OF
TREES
1821
Oil on paper on panel
Royal Academy of Art, London

30. STRATO-CUMULUS CLOUDS
1821
Oil on paper on board
Paul Mellon Collection

31. SKY STUDY
c. 1819
Crayons on blue paper
A. L. Gordon Collection

32. DARK CLOUD STUDY
1821
Oil on paper on panel
Paul Mellon Collection

33. SEASCAPE STUDY WITH RAIN
CLOUDS (NEAR BRIGHTON?)
c. 1824—1825
Oil on paper on canvas
Royal Academy of Art, London

34. THE HAY WAIN
detail of 35

35. THE HAY WAIN
1821
Oil on canvas
National Gallery, London

36. THE CORNFIELD
1826
Oil on canvas
National Gallery, London

37. THE WHITE HORSE
1819
Oil on canvas
Frick Collection, New York

38. THE MELANCHOLY JAQUES
c. 1835
Pencil, ink and wash
Private Collection

39. STUDY OF TREE TRUNKS
c. 1821
Oil on paper
Victoria and Albert Museum, London

40. LANDSCAPE SKETCH ("THE
LEAPING HORSE")
1824—1825
Oil on canvas
Victoria and Albert Museum, London

41. DRAWING FOR "THE   LEAPING
HORSE"
1824
Chalk and ink wash
British Museum, London

42. LANDSCAPE SKETCH (VIEW ON
THE STOUR NEAR DEDHAM)
1821—1822
Oil on canvas
Hallaway College, London

43. DEDHAM VALE
1828
Oil on canvas
National Gallery of Scotland, Edinburgh

REPRODUCTIONS

1. The Valley of the Stour

5. A Country Lane

6. The Gamekeeper's Hut

7. Flatford Mill from a Lock on the Stour

8. View at Epsom

9. Barges on the Stour, with Dedham Church in the Distance

14. The Mill Stream

15. The Mill Stream

17. A Hayfield near East Bergholt at Sunset

18. Self-Portrait

19. Wivenhoe Park, Essex

20. Boat-building near Flatford Mill

22. Maria Bicknell

23. Self-Portrait

26. Flatford Mill on the River Stour

30. Strato-Cumulus Clouds

31. Sky Study

33. Seascape Study with Rain Clouds
    (Near Brighton?)

36. The Cornfield

37. The White Horse

38. The Melancholy Jaques

40. Landscape Sketch ("The Leaping Horse")

41. Drawing for "The Leaping Horse"

42. Landscape Sketch (View on the Stour near Dedham)

44. Dedham Vale (detail)

46. Salisbury Cathedral from the Meadows

50. Landscape Sketch (The Hay Wain)

51. The Valley Farm

52. Water-Meadows near Salisbury

58. Cottage in a Cornfield
59. Cottage at Capel

60. Charles Golding Constable
61. Emily Constable

62. Landscape Sketch (The Valley Farm)

63. Landscape

64. Landscape Sketch (Hadleigh Castle)

ILLUSTRATIONS

Nos. 16, 21, 25, 34, 36, 51, 54, 55, 56
Reproduced by courtesy
of the Trustees of THE NATIONAL GALLERY, LONDON
and Nos. 53, 63
by permission of PREISS & Co., Albaching

MERIDIANE PUBLISHING HOUSE
BUCHAREST

PRINTED IN ROMANIA